STEPS TO SUCCESS

A GUIDE TO EFFECTIVE LIVING

LC GREEN Jr.

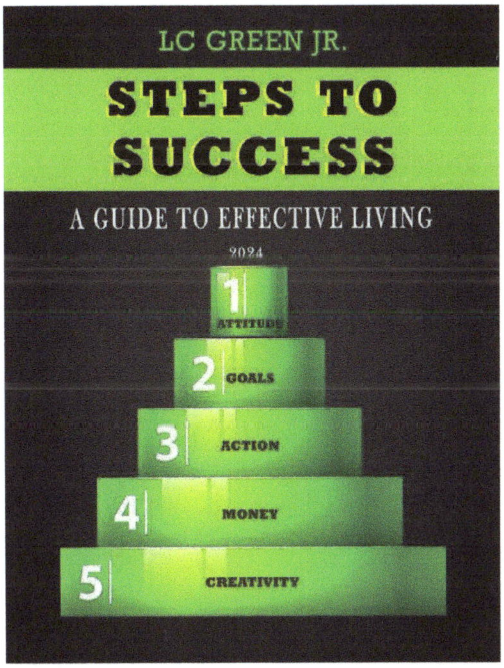

Our Corporate Mission is to Minimize Tax Exposure and Optimize Profitability

Author: **LC Green Jr.**

Published by: **LC GREEN PUBLISHING**

Limits of liability and disclaimer of warranty:
This publication is designed to provide information and education regarding the subject matter covered.
It is sold with the understanding that the author and publishers are not engaged in rendering legal, accounting or other professional services.
If legal advice or other expert assistance is required, the services of a competent professional person should be sought.

LC GREEN JR. PUBLISHING

LC Green & Associates, LLC.

Tax Planners /Wealth Managers

3553 Atlantic Ave. 175

Long Beach, CA 90807

(310) 293-4089

Email: lcgreen@rocketmail.com

ISBN: 979-8-3482-6633-2

For more information on the author and his work, visit him at:

www.lcgreen.com **www.lcgreenbooksforsuccess.com**

Table of Contents

ABOUT THE AUTHOR

Founder of **LC Green & Associates, LLC**., a financial management firm, **LC Green Jr.,** has been in the accounting and financial management fields for more than Thirty-plus years.

As an Instructor at three Los Angeles County colleges for over eight years, Mr. Green has taught Accounting, Bookkeeping, Taxation, and related Financial Management subjects. Mr. Green teaches continuing education for insurance and tax professionals.

He conducts workshops nationwide for major corporations and non-profit organizations and has been an instructor at five colleges in Los Angeles County for over nine years, teaching various subjects such as accounting, bookkeeping, taxation, and other related financial management courses.

As a public speaker LC Green has delivered more than one hundred fifty speeches to diverse audiences throughout the West Coast, with an emphasis on business and personal financial management. Mr. Green is an administrator with the Internal Revenue Service's Taxpayer Assistance Program and the State of California's Tax Preparer's Program.

LC Green Jr. has authored many helpful articles for various magazines, workbooks and newsletters and has published several books including:

- **Steps to Success**
- **A Blueprint for Business Success**
- **How to Avoid / Survive an Audit**
- **How to Use Traditional Marketing Principles in an Online Marketing World**
- **Principles of Business Credit**
- **Learn to do Income Taxes**
- **The Principles of Small Business Taxes**
- **The Principles of Financial Control**

In 2013 LC Green and Associates was Awarded "Business of the Year" by Constant Contact.

For more information on the Author:

email: lcgreen@rocketmail.com

Phone: (310) 293-4089

INTRODUCTION

Based on several studies, one thousand average twenty-five-year-old Americans starting on an equal footing, when asked if they would be successful each will answer "Yes." However, by the time they reach age sixty-five, one will be rich or financially independent, five will still be working, fifty-four will not have money—depending on welfare, relatives, friends, or charity— and the rest will be dead. Out of one hundred people, only five are financially secure. Why is 5% made the grade in the richest country in the world today? Why is there such a wide disparity between what these people intended to do and what they have accomplished?

Only 5% of Americans are considered successful. What is success? Success is the continued pursuit of worthy ideas. If a person is working toward a predetermined goal and knows where he is going, he is a success. If he is not a success, then he is a failure. Success is the progressive realization of a worthy goal.

Think about it. Over nineteen million people in America are sixty-five years old or older, and most of them do not have money and depend on others. Why? We learn to read by the age of seven. We learn to make a living by age twenty-five. However, by age sixty-five we had not learned financial independence in the richest land ever known. Why? It has been stated that the opposite of courage is not cowardliness, it is conformity. We conform. We are acting like the wrong group – the 95% that do not succeed. If most people are asked why they do what they do, they will tell you they do not know. They believe their lives are being directed by outside forces - things they cannot control. They are outwardly directed.

A July 1995 study conducted by CharityVillage.com asked people why they do the things they do. For example: Why do you go to work? Why do you get up in the mornings? Nineteen out of twenty stated they didn't know. Only one out of twenty people knew why they did the things they did. Now, let's go back to our definition of success as working towards a predetermined goal. Success is the person teaching school because that is what he decides to do. It is a salesperson who is selling because that is what he decided to do. A successful person is anyone doing a job because it is what he has decided to do. However, only one out of twenty people is doing that. Why do some people work hard and never seem to get to any place, and others are in the right place at the right time? This is not luck. The 5% of people who make it have goals and attitudes for being successful.

The *"Steps to Success"* is designed to direct you toward understanding the basics of success: Attitude, Goals, Planning, Health, and Faith.

CHAPTER ONE

ATTITUDE

All creatures on Earth - except humans - are being guided by an instinct with which they are unaware, without the capacity to question. However, humans are given the God-like power to create our lives. Every day we put forth actions and ideas that will decide the shape and substance of our tomorrow. For some, those actions and ideas lead to extraordinary achievements and rewards. For some, they lead to a middle ground where a great number of people take their cues from each other, without question or consideration. And for others, those actions and ideas lead to frustration and problems, and they spend their lives at the bottom of the socioeconomic pyramid.

Success or failure as humans is not a matter of luck, circumstance, fate, the breaks, who you know, or any of the other tiresome old myths and clichés that the ignorant use as an excuse. It is a matter of following a common-sense paradigm.

We all want good results in life. The single most important factor that guarantees such results is a healthy attitude. Our attitude is something we can control. We establish our attitude each morning when we start our day. We do just that-whether we realize it or not. It is our attitude toward life that determines life's attitude toward us. We get from life what we expect.

Success is 85% attitude and 15% aptitude. A study by Harvard University revealed that 85% of the reasons for success, accomplishments, promotions, etc., were because of attitude and only 15% because of technical expertise (aptitude). In short, attitude is more important than aptitude. As you undertake a project, your attitude is the dominant factor in its success. William James stated, "The most important discovery of our time is that we can alter our lives by altering our attitudes."

"**Success or failure in business is caused more by mental attitude than by mental capacities**," - Sir Walter Dill Scott.

Through the ages, philosophers have agreed and disagreed on many things, but they all unanimously agreed on one thing: You become what you think about.

In the Bible, we read: "***As a man thinketh in his heart, so is he.***"

There is not much question about it; you will perform the way you see yourself performing. You will be true to your self-image.

"Think on those things which are above, not on those things below." - Colossians 3:2

"All things are possible to him who believes." - Mark 9:23

If you think in negative terms, you will receive negative results.

If you think in positive terms, you will receive positive results.

What you believe yourself to be, you are. Thought is the source of success, material gain, achievement, and fulfillment. Actions are the result of thoughts and feelings that follow action.

Your attitude is the one thing over which you have absolute control. This is one of the most significant and inspiring facts known to man. Attitude control is the result of self-discipline and habit. Either you control your attitude, or it controls you.

There is no compromise. The most practical way to control your attitude is to develop the habit of staying focused on your goals. This is the starting point for the development of the right mindset. Study the life of any man or woman who has achieved success, and you will see that he or she possessed the right attitude, mentally, and directed his or her mind toward reaching definite goals.

The most important motivation you have for changing your self-image is that successful results are produced by the perpetual expectation of attaining them. Despite any natural talents, training, and education, your achievements will never rise higher than your expectations.

Successful people come in all sizes, shapes, ages, and colors, with widely varying degrees of intelligence and education. But they have one thing in common: they expect better out of life than bad; they expect success more often than failure, and they do succeed.

The world in which we live, and work is a mirror of our attitudes and expectations. If we feel our environment could stand some improvement, we can bring about that change for the better by improving our attitude. The world plays no favorites.

It is impersonal. It does not care who succeeds and who fails, nor does it care if we change. Our attitude toward life does not affect the world and the people in it as much as it affects us.

"The mind is the standard of man."- Paul Lawrence Dunbar

Watch what goes into your mind! Your mind is priceless! It is the exclusive source of all you will create spiritually, financially, or materially in your life. Your level of joy, happiness, and peace of mind originates from one place-your mind. Do you protect your mind as carefully as you protect your physical assets?

What if someone entered your living room and told you a juicy tidbit of negative gossip about a mutual friend? Would you listen intently? Would you ask questions to get more details? Or would you toss the person out of your home IMMEDIATELY?

Answer honestly, please. If you are like most of us, you would at least listen politely. You may change the subject as quickly as possible, but you would not stop the person from sharing this type of information.

However, you wouldn't let this same person dump garbage on your floor without becoming enraged! In reality, which behavior is the most detrimental? The garbage a person dumps in our minds is surely far more detrimental than physical garbage that can be easily cleaned up. Most of us have been allowing the dumping of negative garbage in our minds since birth. Think about what you listen to regularly.

"Faith is the substance of things hoped for, the evidence of things not seen."
- Hebrews 11:1

Faith is the prerequisite to positive power. For the individual seeking to develop a powerful persuasive personality, there is no substitute for honest self-evaluation and faith.

Every man or woman must have faith to achieve success. No one can aspire without it. Have faith in yourself, have faith in the Creator. As a rational person knows, there must be a plan and a power controlling the universe. We all are a minute expression of infinite intelligence and, as such, there are no limitations except those accepted in the mind. As a carpenter from the plains of Galilee said, "According to your faith, so be it unto you."

Count as an enemy the person who shakes your expectations of your ability. Remember, self-confidence is the one thing you can never afford to surrender, as nothing multiplies ability like faith in self. It will turn a one-talent person into a success while a ten-talent person without faith will fail.

How often have you heard it said about some successful person: Everything he or she touches turns to gold? We sometimes think of successful people as being lucky. The fact is their success represents their expectation. It is the sum of their habitual ways of thinking. By the force of their expectations, such a person brings success from the most adverse circumstances.

Expectation brings successful experiences, and successful experiences reinforce the power of confidence. A self-reliant, positive, and optimistic person receives "magnetized" conditions. They carry in their very presence an air of victory that compounds their power by convincing others. Their poise, assurance, and ability will increase in indirect proportion to the number of their achievements. Decide right now, today, to be this kind of person. Key points to keep in mind: Success is 85% attitude and 15% aptitude.

As you undertake a project, your attitude is the dominant factor in its success. Your attitude toward others determines their attitude toward you. Treat those you come in contact with as the most important person on Earth. Start this habit and practice it consistently, and you will do it-and benefit from it for the rest of your life.

Before you can make the kind of life you want, you must think, act, talk, and conduct yourself, in all your affairs, as would the person you wish to become. A great attitude is not the result of success.

Success is the result of attitude. PROTECT YOUR MIND! It is your most valuable asset.

CHAPTER TWO

SUCCESS THROUGH GOAL SETTING

The most powerful force for achieving personal success is goal setting. It is goal setting that can move you from dream to reality, from wish to fulfillment, and from conception to consummation. Goal setting gives concreteness to thoughts and translates thoughts into action.

Goal setting begins with the ability to dream. Dreams are the vehicle for identifying possibilities. When you dream, you test possibilities against your desires and adopt those that match. Some dreams are like the wisps of a cloud that provide momentary interest but bring no rain. Other dreams are substantial, enfolding you like a warm cloak on a cold day. They give you purpose and anticipation of tomorrow.

Your dreams shape your future, determine the height to which you shall rise, and bring you the success you deserve. Your dreams and ideas for the future are the basis for the goals toward which you work. What are your dreams? Take the time to write them down. Dreams must be captured, or they slip through your fingers and disappear into the nebulous realm of "might have been." All people have dreams, but most do not have goals.

It is said that only 5% of the people in the world know what they really want to do in life; the rest conceive to be directed by circumstances. Are you going to be in the 5% that choose to live their lives the way they want to live them? If so, how do you translate your dream into action? The way to get a dream into action is by setting immediate and long-term goals.

Long-Term Goals: These are set for where you want to be in a year or more.

Short-Term Goals: These are goals that require immediate attention. The objective of short-term goals is to help you reach your long-term goals. They represent your plans for the next few days, weeks, or months.

Effective Goal Setting

Goal setting is a process by which uncertainties are controlled, and risks are minimized. It is a process by which you decide where you want to go, how fast to get there, and what to do along the way. Goals properly set to chart your course must be carefully defined.

Proper Goals should meet the following criteria. The Goals must be:

1. **Conceivable**
2. **Believable**
3. **Achievable**
4. **Measurable**
5. **Controllable**
6. **Something you really want**

Goals demand creativity. They should be shared only with those who want to see you truly succeed (which would be almost NO ONE you know). Goals must be written.

Why You Set Goals: An individual without goals is like a ship without a captain. The ship may have the finest equipment and structure, yet without a captain to steer and chart its course to a designated port; it goes nowhere and may even drift aimlessly onto the rocks.

Goal setting establishes chief aims. It determines its purpose. Without such aims, our lives will be like an abandoned ship at sea, tossed by the waves of circumstance, often taking the voyage of least resistance.

The key is direction and focus. An individual with specific goals will display determination and drive. Effectiveness and productivity are greatly multiplied when one has a single purpose. Tunnel vision is good when targets are clearly identified.

Goal setting is the initial cause of which success is the final effect.

Goal setting is not a task, but a process; a way of dealing with the world. Several steps are involved, steps that must be repeated as conditions change.

Step 1: **Establish your goals. They must be specific, measurable, time-related, and attainable.**

Step 2: **Establish priority (from most to the least important goals and action steps) and identify potential goals and trade-offs, and how they can be resolved.**

Step 3: **Identify potential goal conflicts and obstacles that could prevent you from attaining your goals.**

Step 4: **Specify the tasks and action steps that must be performed to accomplish your goals.**

Step 5: **Indicate how you measure the results you hope to achieve.**

Step 6: **Establish milestones for reviewing the progress you're making. For example, specific dates on your calendar.**

Step 7: **Identify the risks that are involved in meeting your goals and what must be done to avoid low chances of success.**

Step 8: **Identify and seek the help and resources that may be needed to achieve your goals.**

Step 9: **Review progress periodically, and revise goals and plans as feedback and results indicate that revision is appropriate.**

These are the basic components of effective goal setting. Of course, there are numerous ways of actually going about it. Research and practical experience have shown that these elements are common to almost all successful planning efforts. Become familiar with the process, adapt it to your needs as individually suitable, and begin to practice the approach.

SELF-ASSESSMENT. The first priority on your road to success is realistically evaluating yourself. There is no substitute for being completely introduced to your greatest asset **-YOU**!

Before you can determine where you want to go and how and when you want to get there, you must first know where you are starting. If you must be in New York on the first of next month, you won't buy a plane ticket until you know which city you will be departing from.

This same principle applies to goal-setting and action-planning processes. **Before you can establish your goals and fix your plan of action, you must know where you presently stand.**

If an assessment of your personal qualities and skills shows that you have ample resources for the achievement of the goals you want to reach, you are fortunate. Your pursuit of success is just a matter of determining the best actions to take and then taking them.

If you discover that you need additional skills or personal qualities, you have gained valuable information from your assessment. When you identify the skills and qualities that need to be strengthened or added to your list of resources, it is fairly simple to devise a plan for developing all those qualities and skills.

Personal growth is not always easy, but identifying the necessary action to take is fairly straightforward.

When you know where you stand, you can effectively develop your plan to achieve your goals.

PLANNING THE DESIRED RESULT. ***Planning comes before doing it***. Planning is always as important as doing. The investment of time you devote to planning pays substantial dividends. The will to win is worthless if you do not have the will to prepare.

LUCK IS WHAT HAPPENS WHEN PREPARATION MEETS OPPORTUNITY.

CHAPTER THREE

PUT YOUR PLAN INTO ACTION

THE ACTION PLAN. It is here that you will guarantee your expectations. Thoughtfully answer this question: What is it that I must do each week to accomplish my goals for this year?

You have planned your work, now you must work on your plan. When you meet your goals weekly, your entire year becomes successful. It is here, with each week's activity and results, that the victory is won.

Therefore, you must fix a weekly plan of action that will ensure your success**. A Weekly Effort Formula** becomes indispensable. No patent formula can be developed, which will be adaptable to everyone. The activity necessary for success varies. Likewise, this requirement changes as you gain experience, knowledge, skills, and confidence.

However, it serves your best interest if your activity can be measured against a clearly defined standard. A Weekly Effort Formula, when calculated, can be an extremely helpful self- management tool for you. Building A Weekly Effort Formula, and adhering to it religiously, is the equivalent of having *goal attainment insurance*.

ATTITUDE AND GOALS

The role your attitude plays in goal achievement cannot be overestimated. Goals without the right attitude are not goals at all. The right attitude says, "Yes, I can, and yes I will." And when failure strikes, as it most assuredly will, the right attitude has a fallback position from which it will rally again.

Problems are inevitable, yet through the power of the mind, you can exert a great deal of control over your destiny. According to Napoleon Hill, **"Anything the mind can conceive and believe, it can achieve" and "When you're ready for a thing, it will make its appearance."** His beliefs were based on centuries of empirical evidence drawn from human experience.

The great illusion called misfortune, when viewed rightly, is just that—an illusion. Misfortune and setbacks are often misunderstood illusions because we fail to connect the long-term benefits to the negative occurrence.

"Man is not in the world to set it right, but to see it rightly." - Eric Butterworth

"...And cast now your nets on the right side." - John 21:6

SEEING RIGHT IS THE PASSPORT FROM ILLUSION TO ACCOMPLISHMENT.

Jesse Jackson believes the right attitude will help you reach any star. No matter how adverse your circumstances, how you react (your attitude) is up to you. "Even in the worst situations, you still have the choice between the high road and the low road. It does not take money to buy character, integrity, and decency." Incredible breakthroughs happen once you face your obstacles with the right attitude. The attitude of "I can, and I will" gives you the power and strength to accomplish your goals. One important point to remember: setting goals involves risk. When you set goals, you may succeed. However, you may also fail. If you fail, so what? Risk-taking is inherent in growth, and so is failure. You must be willing to risk failure to succeed.

As Brian Tracy says, "You have to leave the play-it-safe comfort zone and embrace the concept of failure." Make a friend of failure. Use it as a valuable learning experience, a great motivator, and a necessary step on the road to success. At one point or another in their lives, some of the world's most successful people have been miserable failures. Winston Churchill said, "I'd rather fail my way to success than be a successful failure."

Super salesman, Herb True, said, "Successful people often experience more failures than failures do." After Thomas Edison's seven-hundredth unsuccessful attempt to invent the electric light, a New York Times reporter asked him, "How does it feel to have failed seven hundred times?" The great inventor responded, "I have not failed seven hundred times. I have not failed one time. I have succeeded in proving that those seven hundred ways will not work. When I have eliminated the ways that will not work, I will find the way that will work." Several thousand more of these successes followed, but Edison finally found the one that worked and invented the electric light. Success is an attitude. You may fail a great number of times before you succeed. You simply must treat failures as practice shots. Remember the adage: a big shot is just a little shot that keeps shooting.

Keep Trying!

CHAPTER FOUR

LET'S TALK MONEY

"It is the first duty of every man not to be poor."- George Bernard Shaw

"Money doesn't talk, it screams!" - Clara Luper

Men and women have been concerned about money since the first coin was fashioned in Asia Minor, about 750 B.C. You might say that money is like good health, in that we are concerned about it to the extent that we do not have it.

The purpose of this section is to get down to the basics and to clear the air surrounding the entire subject of money. First, let's dispel the old myth once and for all - that money is bad or unimportant. It is not bad. It is definitely important. Money is just as important as food and clothes. It buys shelter. It provides education and pays medical bills. Nothing will take the place of money in the area in which money is needed, and that's certain.

Many Christians and non-Christians, for some reason, cater to the belief that money is evil. Money is not evil. The love of money is evil. The only admonition God gives us is that we must not make money or anything else our God because when we do, we will not be happy. I agree with the belief that God made the diamond folks, and not for Satan's crowd.

To verify this, check the records. Read what God said in Malachi 3:10, Psalms 1:3, and III John 2. You will more than likely agree that money is also scripturally okay.

Solomon was the richest man ever. Abraham had cattle on a thousand hills and Job would not have qualified for food stamps. It is all right to get money—lots of it. As long as you get it the right way - and you do not let money get you.

Keep money in its proper place. It is a servant and nothing more. It is a tool with which we can live better. Money is necessary for modern life. We just need to keep the proper perspective.

MONEY AND SUCCESS

As stated earlier, success is the progressive realization of a worthy goal. Here is how success and earning money works: A person who earns $75,000 a year could be judged as a failure if he is capable of earning twenty-five times that amount. On the other hand, one who earns $19,000 per year could be an overwhelming success if he is using a high portion of his talents and abilities.

Talents and abilities vary, and studies have repeatedly shown that none of us use all our abilities. Very few of us ever use most of our ability. The goal of this book is to convince you that you have more ability than you think and to motivate you to use more of your ability.

Earning money is considered a mark of success primarily because money is a familiar yardstick by which we can measure a contribution. Regardless of what your occupation might be, there are others with the same opportunities who earn considerably less money and others who earn a great deal more.

Remember this formula: The amount of money we earn will usually be in direct proportion to our contribution. ***The opportunity for growth and service lies within the individual***. The more he contributes, the more he will likely earn. Those earning the most money are generally making larger contributions, but there are some obvious exceptions.

For example - the dedicated teacher who chooses to remain in a remote mountain or rural area or a tenement area school because he might be the only hope many of the children have for reaching the bar that has been set for them. Or the devoted doctor who chose to remain in a remote mountain area because he was the only hope for proper health care for miles. Generally speaking, the well-paid teacher or doctor is rendering more service to more people. The same is true for the minister, truck driver, salesperson, etc.

Be realistic about your financial goals. As you reach them, you can then set higher goals. Trying to jump too far too soon can result in confusion, tension, and worry. It is important that you realize your rewards will match your contribution, and you can devise ways and means of becoming the person who is worth the amount of money you establish for yourself.

CHAPTER FIVE

CREATIVITY

"You can be anything you want to be if only you believe with sufficient conviction and act by your faith; for whatever the mind can conceive and believe the mind can achieve."
- Napoleon Hill

Processionary caterpillars follow one behind the other, continuously. During an experiment, a number of them were led onto the rim of a flowerpot forming a circle with no ending. The caterpillars followed one behind the other for seven days until they died of starvation! With food so close.

Like the processionary caterpillars, people, without realizing it, from the habit of playing follow the follower. An example of this behavior is doing things a certain way because it is the way it has always been done without ever considering the possibility that it could be done better.

Just because everyone else is doing things a certain way does not mean it is the best way. Do not wait patiently for success to come to you. Do not assume that others know how to live successfully. Think of a way to do things better.

Ideas come from the mind. Think creatively. Everything comes from creative thinking. There is nothing in this world that has been done perfectly. Everything can be done better. All of today's modern technology was once an idea. The world awaits another George Washington Carver. The magazine industry awaits another John Johnson. Think about ways things can be done better. Put your brain to work to come up with ideas to do things better.

Exercise your brain's creativity. The best way to exercise your brain is to ask yourself questions. For example:

1. **How can I improve myself to become a better person?**
2. **How can I get better with my customers, family, friends, and associates?**
3. **What can I do to increase my value?**
4. **How can I come up with new ideas to advance my business or profession?**

Think about how you can do things better and more completely. You have done important things in the past, and you can do them now and in the future. You can improve your mental capacity by adopting a creative attitude.

Ideas are the starting point of all successes. You never know where your next great ideas will come from or how far they will take you. For most of us, being consistently creative depends on work characterized by concentration and persistence, as well as thinking in a different way.

Creativity is related to variety, which researchers say is the spice of memory. Much age-related memory loss reportedly can be prevented when people seek a great diversity of enjoyable, challenging activities. According to research, here are Twelve valuable maxims for developing a more innovative attitude that helps to stimulate and nurture the creative process:

Establish and Maintain an Open Mind and Spirit of Inquiry

The more you look at things in the same way, the more difficult it is to think about them in any other way. Break out of this prison of familiarity by venturing off the beaten path of your mind. To put it simply: destroy judgment and create curiosity.

Laugh More Because Humor Can Increase Creativity.

According to research studies conducted by Dr Alice Isen at Cornell University, laughter increases creativity and flexibility of thought. So, it can pay to loosen up a bit and have fun while becoming more creative.

Look For Anomalies and Reject Old Explanations.

Learn to approach new challenges and routine experiences with sharpened inquisitiveness. Cultivate the habit of wondering why things work the way they do and whether they should work that way or could be improved. Remember, virtually anything you do can be done in a slightly different, slightly better way.

It Pays To Expect The Expected.

Columbus was looking for India when he discovered America. Alexander Graham Bell was experimenting with a hearing device for the deaf when he discovered the principles of the telephone.

Ask Creative Questions

Creativity and progress depend upon asking the right questions at the right time. Insight-seeking questions help establish a climate in which the creative process can flourish.

Gather Data

In general, the more you know, the more you can create. Get into the habit of noticing what is happening around you, and then ask this question: What is really happening? The creative mind needs facts to draw from, so it pays to be diligent in collecting them.

Let Your Mind Wander

At opportune moments throughout the day, lct your mind shift gcars and wandcr, looking at difficult challenges and routine procedures from odd angles and fresh, unusual vantage points.

Take Time To Play

It may sound odd to suggest that more play boosts creativity and productivity, but it is true. The wondrous human spirit is full of surprises. Rest and relaxation are crucial to productivity. We are obsessed with busyness, but some of the most productive corporate and public figures take time to rest. Mixing in laughter, humor and playing with your work can be a powerful stimulus to the creative process.

Take More Risks and Be Willing to Fail

Being creative is risky. However, it is essential to take risks to be productive. Cultivate the habit of taking chances, of choosing an idea, and allowing the possibility that it may not be the best idea. The person who is willing to propose a new theory suggests a different way of doing things or mentions that the current wisdom might be wrong must be willing to fall flat on his face. AT&T, and other corporations, have even begun issuing "amnesty certificates" to managers and employees, thereby openly empowering them to take risks without repercussions if they fail. We must issue our "amnesty certificates" to ourselves.

Be Goal-Directed, not Goal-Governed

The importance of goals cannot be overstated. Setting explicit and challenging goals is essential to top productivity, but be careful not to carry this too far. Blind pursuit of any one goal may hinder creativity and limit the overall level or quality of your achievement. This is because the course you set may turn out to be the wisest or most fruitful.

You've Got to Get Away

For artists, writers, composers, philosophers, inventors, and entrepreneurs, the spark of creativity has burned most brightly in minds working in solitude. Scheduling time to break away from others and be alone, even for just a few quiet minutes, can open the mind to a new perspective and enable you to reflect more clearly on the challenges and possibilities in front of you.

The Power of Imagination

Imagination is everything. According to Napoleon Hill: "With the aid of imagination, man has penetrated the stars, conquered the sea below and the air above, and created a simpler and easier quality of life by combining ideas and action. The imagination is the great workshop where the potentialities are practically unlimited." Imagination is the key to creativity. Anything that is imagined can be created. Life is a collectivized thought. Imagination is one of the most useful tools you have. Your imagination is the mirror of your soul. Therefore, you have the right to stand in front of that mirror and see yourself as you wish to be.

YOUR IMAGINATION BELONGS TO YOU- USE IT!

CONCLUSION

This is a guide designed to help you reach your goals.

Success has a different definition for each person. What makes one person successful and another a failure depends on what that person's definition of quality of life is. A person can be making all the money in the world, but if he is not happy, he is a failure.

For example today, many people have left lucrative practices as doctors and lawyers to become bakers or artists. These people report being incredibly happy. They realized that money was not the defining element of their happiness—but satisfying their soul's calling.

Use this guide to help you find your soul's calling.

…And enjoy accomplishing your Steps to Success!

lcgreen & associates

WHO WE ARE…

LC Green & Associates Inc. offers a unique team of Financial Professionals with proven expertise in Tax Planning and Wealth Management.

We provide a variety of valuable services that enable individuals and businesses to optimize their profitability and minimize their tax exposure.

LC Green & Associates offers premium levels of assistance and innovative resources for individual and business planning.

PRODUCTS AND SERVICES

At L.C. Green and Associates Inc., we assist in the following areas:

- Tax Return Preparation
- Individual & Business Tax
- Preparation and Planning
- Education
- Income, Gift, and Estate Tax Returns
- Corporation & LLC setups
- Relocation Tax Issues

EDUCATIONAL BOOKS:

- Steps to Success
- A Blueprint for Business Success
- The Principles of Financial Control
- How to Avoid /Survive an Audit
- How to Use Traditional Marketing Principles in an Online Marketing World
- The Principles of Small Business Taxes

www.lcgreen.com Ph: (310) 515 -7316

lcgreen & associates

Tax Planners &
Wealth Managers

Contact Us at:

Mailing Address
3553 Atlantic Ave.
Suite 175
Long Beach, CA 90807

Tax Office
Carson
20411 S. Susana Rd.,
Carson, CA 90810

www.lcgreen.com

(310) 293-4089

LC GREEN JR. of LC Green and Associates LLC. has collaborated with Individuals as well as Large and Small businesses as a Tax Planning and Filing Agency for over several thriving decades. LC also specializes in Tax and Wealth Building, and other Education and Resource Services.

LC Green Jr. is a well-known Author in his community who generously shares his financial success experience through the many books he has written and the notable educational events he participates in – both in person and online.

We hope you have enjoyed the "Steps To Success" advice he has revealed in this book.

For more information you can contact him at:

LC Green Jr. Publishing and LC Green & Associates, LLC.

Tax Planners / Wealth Managers

(310) 293-4089

Email: lcgreen@rocketmail.com